THE TREE THAT TOLD A TALE

THE TREE THAT TOLD A TALE

LISTEN TO THE TREE

DR. JOYCE WILLARD TEAL

Copyright © 2021 Teal's Publishing

All rights reserved. No part of this publication may be reproduced, distributed, or transmitted in any form or by any means, including photocopying, recording, or other electronic or mechanical methods, without the prior written permission of the publisher, except in the case of brief quotations embodied in critical reviews and certain other noncommercial uses permitted by copyright law. For permission requests, write to the publisher, addressed "Attention: Book Rights and Permission," at the address below.

Published in the United States of America

ISBN 978-1-953904-20-1 (SC)
Teal's Publishing
8629 Forest Green Dr. Dallas
TX 75243
www.untealthen.com

Ordering Information and Rights Permission:
Quantity sales. Special discounts might be available on quantity purchases by corporations, associations, and others. For details, contact the publisher at the address above.

For Book Rights Adaptation and other Rights Permission. Call us at toll-free 1-888-945-8513 or send us an email at admin@stellarliterary.com.

Tanza, the Tree, has stood for many years in the church yard of 16th Street Baptist Church in Birmingham, Alabama. Tall and proud, she listened and learned. Now she shares her story for a new generation.

CONTENTS

Introduction xiii

The Beginning 1
The Bombing 4
Accusations 7
More Revelations 9
Lessons to be Learned 10
Glossary of Terms 11
General Facts about Trees 15

Author's Autograph Page

for

The Tree That Told the Tale

This book belongs to:

_____

Is this a gift?

☐ **Yes**

☐ **No**

From:

_____

Author's signature:

_____

Date _____

The Tree That Told the Tale Characters

Barbara Branches

Bob Bark

Lucy Leaves

Linda Limb

Nelson Nest

Randy Roots

Sam Sap

Teresa Trunk

INTRODUCTION

Allow me to introduce myself. My name is Tanza, and I've decided to share my secrets with you. Trees do have secrets. They see it all. Did you know that trees are the longest living organisms on the planet and one of the earth's greatest natural resources? So as you can easily imagine, we see a lot! Did you know that trees keep our air supply clean, reduce noise pollution, improve water quality, help prevent erosion, provide food and building materials, create shade, and help make our landscapes look beautiful? So again, it's easy to recognize why we are desired. And different trees serve different functions. Of course these are not my secrets. All trees know this stuff. Just be patient. I'll get to my secrets in a minute.

THE BEGINNING

As I've already revealed, "My name is Tanza, and I'm a tree." In fact, I'm the lone tree that stands in the church yard of the 16th Street Baptist Church in Birmingham, Alabama. I've given names to my various parts, and you'll meet them as I share my secret with you.

For many years I've stood tall and proud. My leafy branches, which I've named Barbara, have provided shade from the hot sun, shelter from rain, and untold environmental benefits. As the church yard's main attraction, children have climbed me and swung from my branches; some still do, though not nearly as many today as once upon a time.

Ideas have been discussed and crystallized beneath Linda, my limbs, and I was privy to it all. I have witnessed so much, and until now I've kept it all to myself. I never even thought that one day I might want to share my secrets. I never thought about children yet unborn or the young ones who most people would think would not be interested, and certainly the ones who would have no knowledge of the things that I witnessed. For that matter, I always knew that what I'd witnessed had been witnessed by some others, and that in due time, everyone who was interested would probably already know what I knew. And though Barbara Branches, Bob, my bark, Linda, my limbs, Nelson, my lone nest, Sam, my sap, Teresa, my trunk and I knew that *some* others witnessed some of what we did, we always felt, deep within my sap, Sam, that they were our secrets to hold. We felt this way only because we saw what few others saw. We heard what few others heard. After all, people spoke openly in our presence. People spoke as though I, Tanza, wasn't there in the yard absorbing every word. No one ever thought about Ringo, my rings, or what they were privy to as they formed year after year.

But one day, we heard a conversation between two young boys, and immediately recognized that there were probably many children who were interested, just like these two boys; many children who would like to hear the story that only we could tell, a story that these children did not know. After all, while *some* people were there in the yard with me to experience and be witnesses to one of the stories, or maybe even two or three, I suddenly realized that I was the only one there, me, Tanza, the only one in the yard to experience and be a witness to each of the stories as they took place; of each of the events as they unfolded! So we discussed it among ourselves: Barbara Branches, Bob Bark, Linda Limb, Nelson Nest, Randy Roots, Sam Sap, Teresa Trunk and me. And we agreed it was time to tell our story.

For instance, once upon a time the church was bombed and four little girls were killed, and I know who did it! I saw who did it! I witnessed everything that took place on the grounds that morning.

From Nelson's perch near the top, he and Barbara were watching as a man set the bomb in place. My Barbara Branches quivered ever so slightly as Bob Bark heard men whispering to one another. And though I couldn't quite discern their words, I could read their body language, and I recognized that there stealth involved. Had I been able, I would have alerted somebody. I would have called out! But I was a silent observer, up to this point. Remember, I'd never shared my secrets, and never thought I would. We each waited nervously to see just what would happen. We all knew this man was up to no good!

THE BOMBING

You see, the yard of the Sixteenth Street Baptist Church in Birmingham where I stood had always been my home. And this church was used as a meeting-place for civil rights leaders like Martin Luther King, Ralph David Abernathy and Fred Shutterworth. Tensions became high when the Southern Christian Leadership Conference (SCLC) and the Congress on Racial Equality (CORE) became involved in a campaign to register African Americans to vote in Birmingham. Randy Roots reminded me that I should say tension increased, because during this time period racial tension was already high.

But let me get back to my story, the story I now want to share. On Sunday, September 15, 1963, I observed a white man getting out of a white and turquoise Chevrolet car. He placed a box under the steps of the church. Shortly thereafter that morning a bomb exploded, killing Cynthia Wesley, Addie Collins, Denise McNair and Carole Robertson. Each is pictured above.

These four girls had been attending Sunday school classes at the church. Twenty-three other people were also hurt by the blast, but these precious girls were killed.

The bomb also damaged five cars that were parked in the back of the church; completely demolished the back wall, and destroyed every stained glass windowpane in the church, except for one. Surprisingly, this one consisted of Christ holding hands with children leading them to the Promised Land. Although the face of Christ was destroyed, the rest of this stained glass windowpane remained intact. Few of my limbs and branches were damaged, and though the wind produced by the blast blew off a few of my leaves, Lucy, I continued to listen and learn. Sam, Bob and Nelson were very frightened, but they weren't hurt. Linda had a little damage, but not much. I heard discussions that after this horrific tragedy, many white people felt compelled to join the Civil Rights Movement.

ACCUSATIONS

Ringo shared that Civil rights activists blamed George Wallace, who was Governor of Alabama at that time, for the killings. But I knew. Don't forget, I, Tanza, had observed the man put the bomb under the church. But Governor Wallace was blamed because only one week before the bombing, Sam Sap, affirmed that Governor Wallace had told the *New York Times*, "To stop integration Alabama needs a few first-class funerals." So while his sentiments, voiced publicly as they were, might have contributed to this man's actions, the man who put the bomb there under the church is the one who made the choice to do it. Always remember, it doesn't matter what anyone else says, you are responsible for the choices you make! You are responsible for the actions you take! And so was this man!

And though I was a silent witness, another witness, not so silent, identified Robert Chambliss, a member of the Ku Klux Klan, as the man who placed the bomb under the steps of the Sixteenth Street Baptist Church. Chambliss was arrested and charged with murder.

He was also charged with possessing a box of 122 sticks of dynamite without a permit. On the 8th of October in 1963, Chambliss was found *not guilty* of murder and received a hundred-dollar fine and a six-month jail sentence for possessing the dynamite. Remember: four little girls were dead. Their killer had been identified. But all he got was a hundred-dollar fine and a six-month jail sentence for having dynamite. Nelson, my lone nest, shared this with Barbara, Bob, Linda, Sam and me.

This case remained unsolved for many years, and I heard a lot of discussions about it during those years. Then Bill Baxley was elected Attorney General of Alabama. He requested the original Federal Bureau of Investigation (FBI) files on the case and discovered that the organization had accumulated a great deal of evidence against Chambliss that had not been used in the original trial.

Remember Ringo Ring. He learned and shared that in November, 1977 Chambliss was tried once again for the Sixteenth Street Baptist Church bombing. This was now 14 years later, and Chambliss was aged 73. This time he was found guilty and sentenced to life in prison. Chambliss died in a prison in Alabama on the 29th of October in 1985. Ringo also shared, "This means he served less than 10 years. But though justice was delayed, it was not denied."

MORE REVELATIONS

Barbara Branches learned that on the 17th of May in 2000, the FBI announced that the Sixteenth Street Baptist Church bombing had been carried out by a Ku Klux Klan splinter group, the Cahaba Boys. It was claimed that three other men, in addition to Robert Chambliss, had been responsible for the bombing. Listening to discussions held under my branches, sometimes as people leaned against Teresa, my trunk, I heard these men named: Herman Cash, Thomas Blanton and Bobby Cherry. Randy Roots informed me that Cash was now dead, and Linda Leaves shared that Blanton and Cherry were arrested. Bob Bark had learned and revealed to us that Blanton was also tried and also convicted.

LESSONS TO BE LEARNED

I, Tanza, Linda Limb, Teresa Trunk, Barbara Branches, Bob Bark, Sam Sap, Randy Roots and Nelson Nest have shared this story with you. We hope you've learned some things about our history that you did not know. We also hope you have learned the following valuable lessons:

Lesson 1: Justice delayed does not necessarily mean justice denied. You must always do what is right and then be willing to wait for the outcome,

and

Lesson 2. You must always know that only **you** get to make **your** choices. No matter what someone else says or does, you are ultimately responsible for the choices you make and for the actions you take!

GLOSSARY OF TERMS

Accumulated (8):	built up; accrued
Affirmed (15):	verified
Alerted (11):	revealed; made known
Attorney General (16):	the chief law officer of a state
Body language (11):	bodily mannerisms and facial expressions that communicate a person's feelings
Campaign (12):	a planned and organized series of actions
Civil rights activists (8):	persons who actively fight for equal privileges for all
Crystallize (9):	come together; fall into place; take shape
Demolished (14):	destroy completely

Discern (7):	be aware of; tell the difference
Environmental benefits (6):	things that are helpful to our surroundings
Erosion (7):	the gradual destruction, reduction or weakening of something
Evidence (17):	proof; verification
Federal Bureau of Investigation (8):	the chief law enforcement agency in the U.S.
Fred Shutterworth (7):	Civil Rights Leader
Horrific (15):	awful; terrible; horrible
Intact (14):	whole; unbroken; in one piece
Integration (8):	mixing; assimilation
Ku Klux Klan:	a white supremacist organization founded in 1915 in the state of Georgia
Martin Luther King (7):	Civil Rights Leader
New York Times (8):	a major newspaper in that state
Privy (9):	sharing secret knowledge
Racial tension (7):	conflict created between people of different races
Ralph David Albernathy (7):	Civil Rights Leader
Register (12):	get people's names on an official list
Revelation (2):	eye-opener; revealed

Sentiments (8):	feelings; emotions
Splinter group (9):	one segment of a group or organization
Tree sap (9):	liquid produced internally by a tree
Unfold (9):	make known; reveal; become known

GENERAL FACTS ABOUT TREES

- Trees keep our air supply fresh by absorbing carbon dioxide and producing oxygen.
- In one year, an acre of trees can absorb as much carbon as is produced by a car driven up to 8700 miles.
- Trees provide shade and shelter, reducing yearly heating and cooling costs by 2.1 billion dollars.
- Trees lower air temperature by evaporating water in their leaves.
- The average tree in metropolitan area survives only about 8 years!
- A tree does not reach its most productive stage of carbon storage for about 10 years.
- Trees cut down noise pollution by acting as sound barriers.
- Tree roots stabilize the soil and prevent erosion.

- Trees improve water quality by slowing and filtering rain water as well as protecting aquifers and watersheds.
- Trees provide protection from downward fall of rain, sleet, and hail as well as reduce storm run-off and the possibility of flooding,
- Trees provide food and shelter for wildlife.
- Trees located along streets act as a glare and reflection control.
- The death of one 70-year old tree would return over three tons of carbon to the atmosphere.

Printed by Libri Plureos GmbH in Hamburg, Germany